Marissa
Reinert

BLUEBONNET
at
Dinosaur Valley
State Park

To Marissa —

Hope you enjoy this Texas tale

of the armadillo ancestor!

Mary Brooke ☺

Mary Brooke Casad

BLUEBONNET
at
Dinosaur Valley
State Park

Illustrated by
Benjamin Vincent

PELICAN PUBLISHING COMPANY
GRETNA 1990

For Vic, McCrae, and Carter

Library of Congress Cataloging-in-Publication Data

Casad, Mary Brooke.
    Bluebonnet at Dinosaur Valley State Park.

    Summary: Bluebonnet the armadillo visits
Dinosaur Valley State Park and has adventures with
a glyptodon, an armadillo ancestor.
    [1. Armadillos—Fiction. 2. Glyptodon—Fiction.
3. Mammals, Fossil—Fiction. 4. Dinosaur Valley
State Park (Tex.)—Fiction. 5. Parks—Fiction.
6. Texas—Fiction] I. Vincent, Benjamin, ill.
II. Title.
PZ7.C265B1 1990 [Fic]   90-7338
ISBN 0-88289-776-4

Printed in Hong Kong

Published by Pelican Publishing Company, Inc.
1101 Monroe Street, Gretna, Louisiana 70053

Bluebonnet the armadillo had traveled many miles from her home in the Texas Hill Country when she arrived in the town of Glen Rose. She continued her journey, following the signs until she reached her destination—Dinosaur Valley State Park!

At the entrance to the park, Bluebonnet watched as cars stopped at the main gate. Park rangers gave directions to the different camping, picnicking, and sight-seeing areas.

Bluebonnet crept closer and listened. "There's so much to see!" she exclaimed. "But I'll go have a look at the dinosaur tracks first."

Wandering along the winding road, Bluebonnet came to the banks of the Paluxy River. She watched the people stepping from rock to rock to cross over to the other side.

"Hmmmm," thought Bluebonnet to herself, "I think I'll cross the river the armadillo way."

With that, she took a large gulp of air, inflated her stomach so that she would have some air to breathe, and stepped in. She sank several feet to the river bottom, and walked across the riverbed until she came out of the water onto the other bank.

Signs pointed the way to the dinosaur tracks. Bluebonnet shook the water off of herself and scurried along the limestone bank. She stopped at the edge of a huge footprint in the rock.

"Imagine having feet that big!" said Bluebonnet. She thought about the large dinosaur that had made the imprint in what had once been soft mud. "I sure wouldn't want to get in its way!"

Bluebonnet studied the other dinosaur tracks, being careful not to fall in. For a little armadillo, the tracks were like giant craters.

As Bluebonnet turned to leave, she spied a hole in the ground almost hidden between two large boulders.

"Looks like a burrow," she said. "I'll see if anyone is home." Poking her head into the burrow, she called, "Hello?" Her voice echoed: "Hello? hello?" She moved closer to the edge of the hole and called again, but her echo was still the only reply.

Suddenly, Bluebonnet lost her balance. She fell forward into the burrow and began to roll. Her shell curled around her, almost into a complete ball. Faster and faster she tumbled through the dark burrow, unable to stop. Then she hit a large rock with a loud "SMACK," and stopped.

"Ouch!" Bluebonnet cried. "Thank goodness I have a shell, or that would have really hurt."

Her eyes slowly adjusted to the darkness. "This is the deepest burrow I've ever been in," said Bluebonnet. "How am I going to get out?"

To her amazement, she watched as the large rock that had stopped her began to move! "Why, this is not a rock!" said Bluebonnet.

No, the large rock was not a rock at all! In fact, it rather looked like Bluebonnet, but it was much, much bigger. Bluebonnet blinked her eyes.

"Am I really seeing what I think I'm seeing—a giant armadillo?" she asked.

"Oh-h-h!" The giant armadillo yawned and stretched. His eyes opened and shut several times before he fixed his gaze on Bluebonnet.

"What did you call me?" he asked.

"You're a giant armadillo!" exclaimed Bluebonnet. "The biggest I've ever seen!"

"No, I'm not," he replied. "I don't even know what an arma … arma … what did you call me?"

"Armadillo," said Bluebonnet.

"I don't know what an armadillo is. I'm a glyptodon," he said.

"But you couldn't be," said Bluebonnet, shaking her head. "Glyptodons were ancestors of the armadillo. They roamed around Texas thousands of years ago. But they're gone now, just like the dinosaurs."

The glyptodon looked confused. "I must be having a bad dream," he said. "I feel like I've been asleep for a long time."

"Oh, dear," said Bluebonnet, looking startled. "Maybe you have been."

Slowly, the glyptodon got to his feet. He had a shell similar to an armadillo's, but with a large hump in the middle. Another shell extended from the top of his head to the tip of his nose. At the end of his tail was a ball that was covered with sharp spikes.

Bluebonnet gasped in amazement. "You're just like the pictures I've seen," she said. "But I never thought I'd meet a real glyptodon!"

"Well, I'm real all right," he replied. "And I never thought I'd meet such a smaller version of myself—named an armadillo."

Yes, I'm an armadillo—Bluebonnet the armadillo," she said, pointing to her blue sunbonnet.

"I'm Glyndon P. Glyptodon," he said. "But my nickname is Spike." He wagged his spike-covered tail.

Spike looked around the cave-like burrow. "Not much has changed here," he said. "But you say the glyptodons are gone?"

"Yes," said Bluebonnet. "It seems that you have stayed safe and asleep in this cool, dark place for many years. But lots of changes have taken place."

"How strange to be the only glyptodon left," Spike sighed sadly. "But at least I have a descendant of mine with me for a companion."

Bluebonnet smiled. "Are you hungry?" she asked.

"Of course," said Spike. "I'm always hungry." Then he frowned. "Will I still be able to find some plants and insects to eat?" he asked.

Yes," said Bluebonnet. "That's what I eat, too."

"Well," said Spike, looking around, "if I remember correctly, the front door to my cave home is in this direction."

The glyptodon began to walk. Bluebonnet followed. The pathway became lighter and lighter, until they could see the sunlight shining brightly through an opening.

"Why, everything is different!" exclaimed Spike as he emerged from the cave. "The plants and trees are not the same."

Spike nibbled on a leaf. "Not bad," he said.

Bluebonnet started to dig. She found some termites.
"Here, Spike, try these," she said. "We armadillos think they're quite good."

Spike liked the termites that Bluebonnet had provided for him, and ate the whole nest.

"Look here," said Bluebonnet, pointing to a dinosaur footprint in the rock. "Your home is now a part of Dinosaur Valley State Park. Many visitors come here to see the tracks and learn about dinosaurs."

"Ah, yes, the dinosaurs," said Spike. "You mentioned them before. The older glyptondons used to tell us tales of the fierce meat-eater, Tyrannosaurus Rex, and the plant-eaters, Brontosaurus and Triceratops. There was even a dinosaur that had a shell like you and me, an Ankylosaurus."

Spike swung his tail from side to side, showing off the bony spikes on the end.

"Now, the Ankylosaurus had a strong tail, too," he said proudly. "The Ankylosaurus could give Tyrannosaurus Rex a powerful whack with its tail. I used to do the same when the Sabre-Tooth Tiger bothered me."

Suddenly Spike turned around, looking from side to side. "Does the Sabre-Tooth Tiger still live around here?" he asked.

"No," said Bluebonnet.

"Well, that's good … I guess …." said Spike, shaking his head slowly. He seemed lonely and sad. Bluebonnet felt sorry for him.

"Spike," said Bluebonnet, "I came to see Dinosaur Valley State Park. Would you like to explore it with me? Maybe you'll see some places that look familiar."

Spike nodded his head in reply. He walked along the bank of the Paluxy River, leaving his large footprints behind. Bluebonnet followed, making her own tiny tracks in the soft mud. They climbed hills and wandered around trees and rocks.

"This scenery reminds me of my Hill Country home, just south of here," said Bluebonnet.

"It all looks different to me," mumbled Spike. "Nothing is the way I remember it."

Bluebonnet pointed to a pretty blue flower. "This is the bluebonnet, the state flower of Texas that I'm named for," she said proudly.

"That little old thing?" Spike said. "Why, in my day those flowers grew to be three feet tall …"

Suddenly, Spike stopped. "Aha!" he cried. "The dinosaurs are not gone! That looks like a Brontosaurus, and he's in trouble! Tyrannosaurus Rex is after him! Stand clear, Bluebonnet!"

Spike charged ahead. Bluebonnet called after him, "Wait, Spike! Stop!"

Faster and faster sped Spike. Bluebonnet closed her eyes, afraid to look. When she finally opened one eye, she was surprised to see Spike standing still, staring at the dinosaurs before him.

"Bluebonnet!" gasped Spike. "They're frozen."

Bluebonnet scurried over to join him. "They're not real dinosaurs, Spike," she said. "They're statues. In fact, these dinosaur models appeared at the New York World's Fair dinosaur exhibit."

Spike looked more confused than ever. Bluebonnet gave him an affectionate pat with her paw. "Come on, Spike," she said. "There's more to see."

Bluebonnet led Spike down a winding road. They watched as a carload of sightseers passed by.

"Look! A real dinosaur!" cried the children in the car.

Spike let out a roar and hid behind a large rock. "Bluebonnet! What is that? It's as big as a woolly mammoth!" he said in a frightened voice.

The car stopped. Bluebonnet watched the excited children, who were pointing in her direction.

"See the dinosaur? It's a real one!" they said to their parents. But with Spike safely hidden away, all that the parents could see was Bluebonnet.

"Oh, no," laughed the parents. "That's not a dinosaur. That's an armadillo." The car drove away.

"You can come out now, Spike," called Bluebonnet. "It was a car, with people inside of it. It's gone now."

"Car? People? I've never seen anything like it," said Spike, shaking his head in bewilderment.

The two continued along the road until they came to a picnic area. Bluebonnet led Spike to the picnic tables.

"Sometimes you can find food scraps left by the people," said Bluebonnet. "Here, Spike, try some watermelon. It's an armadillo favorite."

"Pretty tasty," said Spike, chomping down on a half-eaten watermelon slice.

The sun was setting. Bluebonnet and Spike watched as other animals joined in the search for scraps.

"What kind of animals are these, Bluebonnet?" asked Spike.

"Well, that's a possum over there," said Bluebonnet, pointing her paw. "And there's a skunk, and a raccoon."

Spike chuckled. "They're pretty different from the animals of my day," he said. "And these people creatures—are they dangerous? Can they hurt you?"

"Some of them can," said Bluebonnet. "We animals have to be careful. But then, you feared the Sabre-Tooth Tiger, didn't you?"

"Yes," said Spike, his eyes growing big. "I certainly did!"

"Yet there were other animals who were your friends," said Bluebonnet. "Well, some people are my friends, too."

Spike appeared to be thinking very hard. "Perhaps," he said, "in some ways, this world is not too different from the one I knew."

Bluebonnet smiled. "Well," she said, "now that we've eaten, how about a cool drink of water from the river?"

Spike nodded. The two friends ambled off together.

Just as they came to the bluff overlooking the river, Bluebonnet and Spike looked down and saw many people gathered by the bank.

"More of those people creatures," said Spike. "What are they doing?"

"Shhhhh!" whispered Bluebonnet. She listened carefully to the voices.

"Now, those little prints were obviously made by an armadillo," said one voice, "but these other footprints don't look like any kind I've ever seen before."

"And they're fresh prints," Bluebonnet heard another voice say. "But they look like they should be hardened in the rock with the dinosaur tracks."

"You don't suppose these tracks were made by some sort of prehistoric animal, do you?" another voice asked.

Bluebonnet watched as the people looked at one another in surprise. Finally, one voice spoke: "Even though it's almost dark, we must try to find the animal that made these tracks. Let's divide into search teams."

"Spike!" said Bluebonnet. "They're looking for you!"

"Me?" exclaimed Spike. "Why do they want me?"

"Well, you are a glyptodon, and until today, I'd never seen one, and neither have the people," said Bluebonnet anxiously. "They're curious."

Spike twitched his tail back and forth. "If the people creatures capture me, what will they do with me?" he asked.

"I'm not sure, Spike," Bluebonnet answered. "But I'm afraid for you. We've got to hide you."

"I stayed hidden for thousands of years in my cave home," said Spike. "Can you help me get back there?"

"Yes," said Bluebonnet. "Follow me."

They moved slowly across the rocks, carefully avoiding the searching flashlights. Once on the path, they hurried along to the hidden entrance of Spike's cave home. Only after they were safe inside did they stop.

"Oh, dear," said Bluebonnet. "That was frightening."

Spike yawned. "I'm starting to get sleepy again," he said. "We've had some exciting adventures today, and after all the years I've been in this cave, I'm not used to it." He looked at Bluebonnet. "What will I do now?" he asked.

Bluebonnet thought for a few moments. "Stay in your cave during the day," she said. "Only come out at night. Other animals will be out, too, like the ones we saw by the picnic tables. They can help you."

Spike blinked his eyes sleepily. "Perhaps I will be all right in this new world, too," he said. "I didn't think I would like it at first, but you've helped me feel at home."

"Spike," said Bluebonnet softly, "I have to leave soon. But I'll stay with you until you fall asleep."

"Thank you, Bluebonnet," said Spike, nodding wearily. "Thanks for everything."

Bluebonnet sang an armadillo lullaby until Spike was snoring heavily. "Goodbye, my armadillo ancestor," she whispered. "I'll not tell anyone that you're here. But if others discover you, I hope they'll be your friends."

And Bluebonnet was off to roam the Texas trails once more.